from you, to you

Tony Cardona

for Daisy: thank you for healing the parts of me that didn't know how to heal <3

note to readers

hey. thanks for picking up this book. whether you stumbled on it by accident or came here on purpose, i'm glad you're here. *from you, to you* is a collection of words i never had the courage (or the right moment) to say out loud. it's broken into five parts:

love,
wounds,
loss,
healing
and finally, you.

some of these pieces are soft. some are messy. some are stitched together from heartbreak and healing. i wrote them as letters i wish i could've sent—but maybe they were always meant for someone like you.

before you dive in, i want to give a gentle heads up:
this book contains themes of depression, suicide, grief, domestic violence, and physical + emotional abuse. nothing is written with the intent to shock as it's all from lived experience, and i've done my best to handle each topic with care. if you're not in a space where you feel safe reading certain things, please listen to yourself first. skip a page. close the book. come back when you're ready. or don't. that's okay too. and if you ever need someone to reach out to, i've included a list of resources in the back of the book, just in case.

these poems began with what came from others — love, hurt, loss — but in the end, they circle back as something i can finally offer to you.

above all, this is a space for honesty. and i hope, in some way, it helps you feel less alone.

thanks for reading.
really.
– tony

contents

to my first love

i.

oftentimes, the world blares with too much noise
especially during the moments
when silence is the only sound i desire

there's always a chaotic mix of noises around me:
honking horns from impatient drivers
sirens that go in and out of range
dogs playing a game of *'who can bark the loudest?'*
babbles over breakfast
and murmurs over morning headlines

and then-
you step into view

we bridge the moment with our eyes,
silence blankets all the noise,
and the rumble of the world completely recedes

the horns turn into a hush that feels heavier than sound
the sirens turn into stillness between heartbeats
the barks turn into breaths that settle into our bones
and the murmurs turn into moments
that dream the world away

as the seconds stretch and soften,
the sun persuades the earth to sit still just for us,
so even the day can learn what love looks like

for far too long, i surrounded myself with people
who worsened my mental health

my feelings were never valid,
my flaws were always pointed out
their happiness was a weight i ended up carrying
and i felt like i would never be good enough

but with you,
my mental health has skyrocketed
you listen without judgment,
you make me feel *heard*
you let my creativity flow
and became the voice my silence needed

there are many things i can say about you,
but the one that gives me the most peace
is very simple:

you are what my mental health needed

i was a broken seashell,
worn down by the storms around me

you were the ocean that refined me
until i shimmered like treasure

you taught me how to love myself,
and that has allowed me to love you even more

what made me fall in love with you? well...

when we first started working together
at that amusement park,
i never would have guessed that the roller coasters around us
weren't what gave me the thrill of a lifetime.
our paths kept crossing in not-so-coincidental coincidences
until they eventually converged
and created one beautiful path.
by the time i noticed i was falling,
i had already fallen for you.

i fell in love with the way your eyes glistened in the sun,
like two planets shining for the whole universe to see.
i fell in love with the way your laugh
danced with my eardrums,
and how it never ceased to make my laugh dance as well.
i fell in love with how safe i felt in your arms,
as they were the only place i felt genuine peace
in the midst of chaos.
i fell in love with how emotional you got
over the simple things in life,
as it made me appreciate every aspect of life
much more than i ever had before

you changed me,
in the most beautiful way.
you changed the way i see the world.
you taught me to believe in myself.
you gave me a shelter every time it rained.
you watered the parts of me i hadn't bothered to check up on
for years.
you transformed me from the worst version of myself
into someone i never thought i could be.

life really *is* like the roller coasters we used to ride:
it's shaky at times,
unpredictable,
and sometimes too fast to hold on to.
but with you by my side,
it's a ride worth taking,
and a life worth remembering.

as our story unfolds,
we're building a home
for our souls to fall into
not with bricks,
but with glances and shared memories

we're building a living room
with couches that remember our laughter
and mugs that rest on mismatched coasters

a bathroom where your mascara stains the sink
and the mirror takes daily screenshots

a bedroom lit by your fairy lights
filled with dreams that slowly become real

a roof placed by God Himself
sturdy in the winter,
soft in the summer

no matter how hard life gets for us,
we'll always have a shelter when the world storms in,
and a house that actually feels like *home*

i thought i understood what love was
until i met you,
and you taught me there was so much more to it

i believed love was hiding notes
in the places you'd least expect but always find
or bringing you an iced chai tea latte
because you said it tasted *just like fall*
or wrapping my jacket around your shoulders
before you even admitted you were cold

while these are examples of loving gestures,
they are mere stars
in the galaxy that is love

love is staying up all night to comfort you while you are sick
love is walking through your worst moments with you,
even when you push me away
love is supporting your dreams,
even if it means sacrificing mine

for me,
our love became real
the moment your needs
outweighed my own

falling for you wasn't part of the plan,
and i never imagined
that so many blessings
could come from silence instead of answers
but sometimes,
unanswered prayers
are the ones that guide us home

do you remember the first time i told you i loved you?

it was new year's eve,
and rain was falling all around us.
anticipation dawdled in the air,
but it wasn't for the clock striking twelve.
we locked eyes,
and a silent current sparked between us,
carrying nervous excitement across a space not yet crossed.
before we knew it,
the current shortened and our lips met for the first time,
a feeling both soft and electric
as the rain around us danced like it knew.

it felt as if time created a private universe for us
just so we could savor our moment.
after our lips parted ways,
there was a lingering feeling in the air,
an unspoken promise
as the rain continued to dance around us,
sealing this memory forever.
we didn't know it then,
but that moment was the beginning
of the greatest love story ever told.

your precious eyes are portals
to a world i only dreamed of being invited to

your lovely laugh is a melody
created specifically for my soul to dance to

your loving heart is vast and unselfish,
like an endless ocean that feeds every river,
yet never runs dry

your endless kindness is soft and nourishing,
like gentle rain that falls for flowers waiting to bloom

your tender soul is strong and resilient,
like a flame that refuses to be quenched
despite the wind that encompasses it

and your entire being is like fire
not the kind that destroys,
but the kind that warms my entire soul
you are candlelight that never goes out,
a bonfire in the middle of winter,
a fireplace that softens and kindles

you are you,
and that's what i love most about you

our love story is the kind of story
people write books about

we're living every page
as if it's being written in real time
except our love isn't confined
to text between two slabs of pressed wood
because no spine could bear the weight
of ink seeping through every page

our love is more than just a story
it transcends words and life itself

i spent years praying
that i would find someone to treat me right.
praying that i would stop falling into the same cycle of toxicity
i trapped myself in.
praying that i could finally find peace with someone
instead of receiving turmoil in return.
i questioned why God kept saying *no*,
but really,
He was saying *not yet*.

my prayers weren't unanswered.
God just waited to answer them until the time was right.
if He had sent you my way earlier,
we may not have been ready for our paths to cross
when they needed to.
instead,
we met at the exact moment we were supposed to meet,
and peace finally made room for us both.

i spent years chasing love with no foundation

i chased love that surfaced in the light
but disappeared at night,
yet wondered why I never felt bright

there was a hunger inside of me that words couldn't feed,
and that's because i could only be nourished by one person:
you

my past relationships didn't work out
because they were leading me toward you
you didn't just stay,
you gave my soul a home

they warned me love would be hard,
but with you,
love feels just like breathing

i used to dread mornings
and refused to change my routines
but now,
i eagerly set alarms
so i can catch the sunrise with you

it's amazing how love has a way
of making the difficult feel natural

i didn't notice how much i was being weighed down
until you stepped into my life

i was anchored by an excess of anxiety, bitterness, and anger
and still questioned why my ache felt so heavy

the first time you spoke my name,
the weight inside of me lifted

you were the current that loosened the anchor's grip
and my soul was finally able to breathe again

there are many decisions people make
that will alter the course of their lives

your living space
will impact the quality of your life
your lifestyle habits
will impact the length of your life
your financial decisions
will impact the stability of your life

before you know it,
the life you live
is the one you built

and yet,
the most important decision of *my* life,
who to spend it with,
was a decision i never even had to make

it was always you,
and it was *yes* from the very beginning

when we go to the beach
and listen to seagulls argue with each other
while the water plops and splashes in the background,
it feels like home

when we visit carnivals
and see children walking around
with prizes bigger than themselves
and hear screams filled with utter fear and pure joy,
i finally feel known

when we go on road trips
down snaky country roads,
singing out-of-tune songs
(and getting the lyrics all wrong),
it feels like home

when we stop by coffee shops
and inhale the scent of wood and coffee beans
and the trace of deep conversations in the air,
i no longer feel alone

when we host picnics in the woods
and partake in the natural beauties of life
with the taste of lettuce tattooed on our tongues
and the sound of wildlife pulsating in our ears,
it feels like home

no matter where we go,
i will always feel at home
because to me,
home is any place with you in it

for me, demonstrating true love
isn't about the big gestures,
like the dreams you forget
as soon as you wake up

true love is about the little things you do,
but think i don't notice

like the way you remember
exactly how much sugar i take in my coffee
or how you squeeze my hand
when i look for reassurance

it's in the way you check in on me
the moment my eyelids open for the day
and how you listen not just to my words,
but to all the meaning behind them

true love is shown
when your lips don't move
but you still say *i love you*

the sound of your laughter
is a sound i want to share with you
for the rest of my life

it is as soothing as the *pat-pat-pat*
of rain tapping on a window
after a long drought

it is as calming as the *crackle*
of a bonfire in the middle of summer

it is as relaxing as the *whoooosh*
of a breeze in the middle of a hot day

every time i hear the sound of your laughter,
i feel like a child again,
and my inner child giggles at your side,
catching up on years' worth of missed laughter

i am enamored
with the way the life itself
feels *different* when i'm around you
joy comes naturally
burdens become easier to carry
and even sad moments feel less lonely

you opened the door to my heart
and let it run free
opened my eyes to things i could not see
and put faith into things i could not believe

you are the breeze
that reminded my lungs
how to breathe again

falling for you feels like stepping into sunlight
that doesn't burn
after spending a lifetime in the shadows

it feels like the first sip of water
that tastes like hope
after spending years stranded in the desert

it feels like sinking into a fresh mattress
that absorbs all my pain
after weeks sleeping on a bed of nails

falling for you feels like finally being at *home*
in a place i had always been
but never felt i belonged

ii.

i spent far too long searching for you in other places

i looked for you
in the way petals wait to be kissed by morning dew

i looked for you
in the way sand asks the tide to meet it,
even if just for a moment

i looked for you
in the way snowflakes are held by warm hands,
at the cost of their existence

and in the process of looking for you,
i didn't even notice
i was beginning to lose myself

before,
my heart would race when your fingers brushed against mine,
politely asking to be interlocked

it would jump with joy every time your name flashed
across my phone screen

it would pound with eagerness
when it wondered if yours felt the same way

but now,

it stays silent, knowing the only thing
my fingers can hold
is the air we used to share

it wilts every time i hear a chime,
and it isn't from you

and my heart sinks like an anchor
hoping that yours still beats for mine,
unsure if it ever will again

i thought you truly loved me,
and you did at first,
but it wasn't *true* love
because *true* love stays
no matter how shaky the sky turns

anyone can stay when everything is easy,
but people who *truly* love one another
withstand all the tribulations that surround them,
even when storms try to tear them apart

but in the end,
you were simply a parachute
that only opened in ideal conditions
you loved me when the air was still,
but the moment the air howled,
you refused to open up for me,
letting me

plummet

into

grief.

i was supposed to spend the rest of my life with you. we were supposed to go to sleep every night together and wake each other up with the smell of coffee. we were supposed to start our own traditions, like tuesday movie nights and yearly gift exchanges. we were supposed to explore the world together and create photo-album memories that we could look back on when our hair turned a little whiter. instead, i   watched   you slowly   drift   away   from   me.   in   the   process, you   took   all   of   my   desires   with you,   leaving   me   surrounded by   dreams   with   no   one to   share   them   with.

to be honest, i don't trust you

alarms ring in my head,
telling me what i already know,
yet i purposely ignore it

if the eyes are the window to the soul,
your phone is the window to your world,
and i refuse to take a peek at it,
not out of respect for your privacy,
but because i'm terrified of what i might find

the horror of uncovering whatever may be hiding there
is enough to keep me smiling through suspicion

when you quickly moved on to someone else,
you cracked my ribcage open
and walked away with my heartbeat.
it was the ultimate betrayal.
i lost a part of myself and had to watch it love someone else.
it felt as if i'd been walking through a desert
in the scorching sun,
and when i finally saw a jug overflowing with water,
it was locked behind bulletproof glass.

an enormous weight has developed inside my chest.
a massive cloud of lost desire
drowns my lungs with disappointment.
i want,
no,
i *need* to figure out what went wrong and why.
was it something i said?
or something i never found the words for?
or something i never saw coming?

anger and resentment surround me
like a swarm of angry hornets,
demanding justice at first
but then settling for a simple explanation.
loneliness has enveloped me and trapped me in its embrace
and has removed my ability to trust anyone.
a thousand voices surround me,
but not one speaks my language.

you were never something i owned.
but you still felt like something i lost,
like i was writing a love letter
to someone whose address i misplaced.

you stood up for strangers online,
yet let me take the fall in my own living room

maybe if you fought *for* me
the way you protect everyone *but* me,
we would still be together

but instead,
you turned into the very storm
you told me to stay away from.

at the beginning, our love held lightning in our hands
your beauty plucked my breath,
your excitement was infectious,
and our adventures ran wild through my bloodstream,
but little by little, everything began to feel hollow

the love we shared between us
slammed from first gear into reverse without warning
and the silence that followed
felt louder than any ride ever was

the compliments that used to give me butterflies
became stale
a cup once overflowed with love
is now collecting dust
late-night drives and calm sunday mornings
faded into memories that would never be revisited

eventually,
we became strangers who shared memories,
but nothing more

were you my right person at the wrong time? i mean, i gave my everything to something that amounted to nothing.

your absence crushed my soul a little more each day and my hope for love faded into transparency.

i crumbled under the burden of our relationship. arguments became part of our routine, the distance between us expanded, and love turned into something we kept track of. every compliment just felt like a disguised apology.

but it wasn't always like that.

i felt at home with you. your laughter was therapy for my heart and your presence was warmth for my soul. you unlocked a part of me i didn't even know existed.

it was easy to fall in love with you. you were drop-dead gorgeous externally and even more precious internally. your *hello* woke the butterflies inside me. every touch, kiss, conversation, and gesture was a gentle push toward healing the cracks in my heart.

so i ask myself once again, were you my right person at the wrong time?

(now start at the bottom, and climb back to the top)

i think i'll always love you

you left a permanent tattoo on my heart
in the shape of your name
and though i wish i could stop loving you,
my mind is now a compass
that only points toward you

it feels as if the harder i try to forget you
the more i think about the good times we shared,
even though tears outweighed laughs

i think i'll always love you,
and i don't know if that's what will keep me going...

...or break me in ways i won't see coming.

find the difference between these two lists:

- an abandoned city
  with no buildings
- a rainy day
  that never ends
- a picture with the color
  drained away
- a wilted flower in
  a forgotten vase
- a puzzle with one
  missing piece
- a book that ends in the
  middle of the story
- a birthday candle
  with no flame
- a night sky
  with no stars
- a single set of footprints
  in the sand
- an empty chair
  during every meal

- visiting famous landmarks
  in person
- an exquisite masterpiece
  in an art gallery
- a garden
  in full bloom
- a handwritten
  love letter
- a home i never want
  to leave
- laughing
  until my cheeks ache
- the first bite
  of my favorite dessert
- the perfect breeze
  on a morning day
- the aroma
  of morning dew
- warm coffee
  on a winter evening

have you found it yet? no? it's quite simple, really. the
difference between these two lists is.....

......fate.

my therapist, echoing tennyson, said,
it's better to have loved and lost than never to have loved at
all,

but what if i never wanted to love at all?

what if my desire to love and be loved
is the foundation for all my despair?

is it possible to avoid losing
by avoiding love in the first place?

after all, had i not fallen in love,
there would be nothing to miss.

right?

...right???

you held my hand and said you'd never let go, but...
here i am holding on to nothing.

sharing laughs with you gave my heart a home, but...
eviction notices come without warning.

i seized every *i love you* you gave me, but...
love slipped through the cracks anyway.

i really thought we were going to last forever, but...
our *always* didn't last.

love is the most powerful force on the planet
and it is always worth fighting for
as long as you're not the only one fighting

a bridge with only one side isn't a bridge
it's just a broken crossing

and if you're fighting for love,
but you're the only one throwing punches,
you're not *really* fighting for love

you're just fighting to keep yourself from losing
even though you've already lost

what you say:

i just need
some space

i miss the way
we used to be

i don't want
to lose you

can we please
talk about this?

i'm tired of
fighting for us

what i hear:

you're already stepping
away for good

we'll never
get back there

you're letting me
go now

by now, you've
made up your mind

you've decided i'm not
worth the fight

my therapist said,
a broken heart is a chance to start over,

but what if i'm tired of starting over?

what if i'm tired of walking toward a goal
that seems farther away
the more progress i make?

all the pain.
dried tears.
long days.
empty desire.
self-doubt.

am i really supposed to just throw it all away
and start over?

act like none of it really happened?

if i do that,
won't it mean that all the suffering i underwent
was for nothing?

iii.

how to nourish your heart

<u>a recipe for the heart and mind</u>

ingredients:
2 cups unwavering support
1 heaping spoonful of kind words (for yourself and others)
1 gentle drizzle of patience
3 tablespoons forgiveness (one for yourself, two for others)
1 pinch of understanding (add as needed)
2 scoops quality time with loved ones
1 gallon self-care

instructions:
1. in one of your safe spaces, mix unwavering support
   with kind words until they start forming trust.
2. slowly stir in patience, especially where self-doubt
   has crept in.
3. add forgiveness, one tablespoon at a time.
   allow it to fully dissolve before moving on.
4. add a little understanding and make sure to mix
   with an open heart.
5. pour the scoops of quality time and let everything marinate.
6. gently add self-care and ensure it covers *everything*.
   this is the most important ingredient.
7. let everything marinate for as long as you need it to,
   allowing love to rise and settle naturally.
8. serve daily, with gentle reminders that you are enough.

enjoy warm, often, and without guilt.
give it freely to those who love you,
but always serve yourself first.

our story was unforgettable,
and it left its fingerprints all over my life

it started off as a fairytale,
one where our lives were woven together by fate

we grew closer as we shared moments of joy,
passion, and vulnerability

just when i thought things couldn't get any better,
they couldn't get any worse,
and our castle crumbled into a haunted house

we started arguing about everything,
each argument slowly unraveling what we had
we tried to stitch love's torn seams,
but sadly,
there was nothing left to mend

we may not have had the ending we wanted,
but we got the ending
that unlocked the door to new beginnings

although we didn't end up together in the end,
we wrote some chapters worth remembering,
and i'll hold on to the good,
despite the cracks it left behind

not every love is meant to last,
but some lead us to the right one

you weren't the home i'd grow old in,
but you taught me how to breathe again
in the quiet moments over morning coffee

because of you,
i know love is never wasted,
even when it leaves

Tony Cardona

we weren't meant to be,
and that's okay
our story was short
but still worth telling,
and there's no shame in turning the page

a broken kite
doesn't take away from the fact
that the sky is just as beautiful from the ground
even a broken kite still flew for a while,
and we were worth that flight

i'm glad we didn't end up together

when we first broke up,
i couldn't understand why the pain after you
was sharper than the pain with you,
even though i struggled to *survive* while i was with you

i'm not happy about what happened between us
i wish i didn't have to deal with
so much emptiness and betrayal,
but i am grateful,
because among all the uncertainty and the chaos
i gained valuable knowledge about boundaries
and walking away,
lessons that only heartache could teach

when i changed my perspective on our story,
it became much easier to understand
i don't see our relationship as *over*
i see it as *completed*

a *game over* screen feels like failure
but a *game completed* screen feels like closure
and our relationship faded into credits
as our story concluded

we did what we could
we had some really good times together
and just as many bad times
the only thing we can do now
is close the chapter
and watch the credits glide
knowing every mission was complete

the more i dwell on it,
the more i realize that you were never the love of my life

the love of my life would treat me like her crown jewel,
she would be my anchor when waters became rough,
her words would wrap around me like warmth in winter

but you?
you treated me like a placeholder
you left me stranded in the middle of the ocean
you introduced a storm of insults and called it love

the love of my life would do everything she could
to shape me into an exquisite masterpiece
you did everything you could
to whittle away at me until i was nothing but shards

you're not the love of my life
because the love of my life would know my worth,
even on my worst days,
and she would never put herself in a position to lose me

if the depth of my love was that deep for the wrong person,
imagine the depth of love i'll have for the right person

i gave everything i had in my last relationship
and it still wasn't enough
the weight of holding on
became too much to handle
and i was trapped in a cloud of self-blame mixed with doubt
but amidst all the crashing waves,
i could see open water again

my past losses are not failures
they are a demonstration of my capacity to love

the journey i have travelled thus far,
although painful at times,
led me to where i stand today

i can see still water ahead of me,
and as long as i keep moving forward,
i know the tide will carry me to safe shores

i focused so much on being the protagonist in your story
that i forgot to be the protagonist in my own

i kept trying to force myself where i didn't belong,
and it was as pointless as watering a dead garden
expecting it to come back to life

i was never going to be
more than a supporting character in your chapter
so in order to bring the focus back on myself,
i had to accept that i already played my part in your tale
and that didn't mean i had to stop writing mine

and suddenly,
i picked up the pen again
not to edit your lines,
but to write my own

and my story continued to unfold
with the one i'd been neglecting all along

when we first fell in love, i inhaled purified air after spending months breathing polluted air. our love felt fresh, original, and full of unlimited promise. warmth returned to my heart after being frozen with resentment for years.

at its peak, our love was intense. it felt vibrant, all-consuming, and indestructible. i was finally at peace with my life, but that peace only lasted so long, because i could hear the distant mumble of thunder getting closer by the second, and the rainstorm was quickly approaching.

as fast as lightning strikes, our love shifted, and slipped away. our leaves fell too quickly, and i couldn't pick them all up in time to save us. before i knew it, our summer ended in a single burst of fireworks: brilliant, but gone in the dark.

the coldness of love was excruciating. i felt betrayed, i felt lonely, and i entered a state of numbness i never thought i would enter. i couldn't understand how we went from a garden in full bloom to a desert left cracked and dry.

now, i have a new sense of renewal. the coldness was a necessary rest before i could grow again. i am comforted by the thought that love will always return in some form. as for me? spring isn't just coming; it's blooming inside my chest.

to the ones who hurt me

i.

i'm playing tug-of war with you
except you've got a team behind you
and i'm pulling alone
you always talk about meeting each other in the middle,
but if we always do what *you* want,
is it really meeting each other halfway?
or is it just you moving the middle closer to your side?

if the sky promises sunshine
but drowns the day in darkness,
will the earth trust its forecast?

if a compass claims to point north
but always leads south,
will the wanderer still follow it?

if a storyteller promises the truth
but fills pages with castles that never stood,
will the reader still believe him?

so when you repeatedly told me partial truths,
why did you expect me to fully believe you
when your footsteps never matched your words?

looking back on it all,
i can't say that i was happy when we were together
you only gave me happy moments
and i confused the two for far too long

i smiled the day you brought me flowers,
but ignored the months before
when tears were part of my morning routine

my heart felt lighter
when you gave me compliments and reassurances,
but your words grew burdensome,
sharp enough to pierce beneath my skin

though i felt happy at times,
i can't say i was truly *happy*
if anything,
my darkest seasons
began and ended with you

i am tiptoeing through an endless minefield
where any wrong step can lead to an explosion
of tangled emotion
i'm never sure what i could set off at any given moment,
sacrificing my own comfort and peace
just to avoid upsetting you

i feel like a kid again
terrified to disappoint my parents,
doing everything i can
to earn their pride
but it's not for sale

i love you so much,
i really do,
but is that because i genuinely love you,
or because i'm absolutely terrified of you?

you bring out the worst in me. that's on you.

i didn't yell because i'm angry. i yelled because i care.

you're lucky i stayed instead of walking out.

my parents never hugged me. i don't know where to start.

maybe if you were easier to love, i'd know how.

you restrict growth
by avoiding responsibility
and making others carry *your* guilt

every excuse you throw
only delays the inevitable,
like paint on a wall that's already collapsing
covering your cracks with blame
won't stop your foundation from crumbling

you struggle to find solutions to your problems
because you constantly delay the inevitable

it's like adding water to soap
to create a seemingly endless supply
over time, the soapy water won't even help clean
it'll just be dirty water

your problems won't magically disappear by ignoring them
because one day,
the sink will overflow
and you'll be ankle-deep in the mess you tried to avoid

how do you expect me to believe that you love me
with all of your heart
if you only show it half the time?
you've made me settle for love with missing parts
as if that's all i deserve

one day, you're affectionate and loving
the next, you're distant and uninterested

your love only fits into the gaps in your schedule,
and you refuse to make room for me,
even when i need you

you can't love me with all of your heart
only on your terms,
because if you only half-love me,
you don't love me at all

the only thing worse
than loving someone who is toxic to your health
is falling in love
with a version of them that doesn't exist

a *real* person
cannot love you in the same way
that someone who doesn't exist can
and when your mind combines the two,
your heart learns to mistake the wound
for the cure

why didn't i leave you despite living in hell?
because i genuinely thought i was in heaven

i believed that your toxic actions
were a normal part of every relationship
and i just had to learn how to deal with them
i didn't know i was in a toxic relationship
until i realized heaven wouldn't make me this afraid

i was lucky enough to leave the situation when i did,
because too many of us drink poison
believing it's water,
and we don't notice it's killing us
until it's too late

your trauma may have explained your behavior, but it didn't
excuse it. i understand that you had a rough upbringing, and i
wish you never had to endure all the turmoil you experienced,
but that doesn't make what you did to me okay.

you had a chance to end your generational cycle.
the decision to cut it off was in YOUR HANDS.
but you dropped the weight of your world onto mine,
and i suffocated.

you knew exactly what it felt like to be a victim. you knew what
it was like to live in the same cycle of fear, self-doubt and
emotional exhaustion. you knew exactly how past actions
shaped present behaviors, yet you chose to pass on the victim
role to me.

you should've done everything in your power to heal me.
instead, you did all you could to break me.
and it worked.

when will we start holding abusers accountable
for their actions?
too often, abusers walk free.
victims carry the weight of actions that were never their fault.
and far too often,
abusers are protected,
as excuses replace consequences.
if we held them in check instead of enabling them,
maybe victims wouldn't feel so helpless.

why do we ask victims why they stayed,
instead of asking abusers why they hurt?
if it was so bad, why did you stay for so long?
are you sure it was that bad?
why do you keep going back?
we need to stop blaming victims for 'staying',
and start asking abusers
why they made 'leaving' the only option.
why did you hurt her for so long?
how could you not see the damage?
why do you keep hurting him?

why are people taught to avoid abusers,
but not taught how to never be abusive?
inherently, we are taught survival,
but rarely is the focus on prevention.
if we taught people how to be respectful,
how to show empathy,
how to take accountability,
survival wouldn't be as necessary.
of course it's important to learn how to survive.
but it's even more important
to stop putting people in situations
where survival is the only option.

how many people have stayed silent,
not because they had nothing to say,
but because they feared their pain would be questioned?
many victims refuse to speak out
because the weight of judgment
is sometimes heavier than the pain itself.
they are blamed.
judged.
outcast.
all for surviving someone else's turmoil.

we need to break the shield for cruelty that is silence.
we need to shatter the chains of blame that restrict justice.
we need to make space for the silenced to speak.
we had our time to talk.
now, it's time to listen.

perhaps the most beautiful creation on this planet
is clay

it is soft and full of promise
it is pure and holds the ability to take any shape
hands can press, mold, and sculpt it
into quite literally anything

but sadly, many times, clay does not choose its form
forceful hands press too hard
and shape it into something unnatural,
something it never wanted
the hands reshape it at will,
ignoring its cracks,
its silent protests

in some instances,
it dries too fast
in others,
it crumbles under the weight of everything before it

the hands claim control
and don't allow the clay to realize its true form
it could be free,
it could be graceful,
but the hands force it into a shape
it never imagined for itself

the clay molds into sorrow
because although it stands on display,
praised by strangers who only see the surface,
it never feels like itself

do you think physical violence makes you strong?
tough?
powerful?
because it's actually the weakest thing you can do,
a mask to hide how small you *really* feel

you can't hold the chaos inside,
so you throw it at the world around you,
and every time you try to conceal who you are,
you reveal more than you ever wanted me to see

*you're so beautiful, YOU'RE BEING TOO SENSITIVE, i love
your smile, YOU'RE LUCKY I PUT UP WITH YOU, you have
the most amazing eyes, YOU ALWAYS RUIN EVERYTHING,
you make me so happy, YOU MADE ME DO THIS, i'm so
lucky to have you, YOU WOULDN'T LAST A DAY WITHOUT
ME, you're the best thing that ever happened to me, YOU'RE
BEING TOO DRAMATIC, you're absolutely perfect, YOU
CAN'T DO ANYTHING RIGHT, i love everything about you,
YOU'LL NEVER BE GOOD ENOUGH, YOU SHOULD BE
GRATEFUL I'M WITH YOU*

i heard every word you said,
but i listened to some better than others

maybe if you understood how your words affected me,
you would change how you use them

*(but let's be honest,
if you really cared about the way you used your words,
you would've silenced yourself long ago.)*

i got too comfortable
with things that were not normal
i wanted to see my bruises and scrapes
as battle scars of everything i overcame
but truthfully,
they were just marks of shame and guilt,
carved quietly into my skin

i kept telling myself
at least it wasn't as bad as last time
and that's how the bruises darkened
and the scratches bled longer

my therapist said,
be yourself because everyone else is taken
but what if i don't want to be myself?
what if i'm tired of wearing the same skin for so long?
what if i want to be anyone *but* myself?
what if being someone else
exchanges my uniqueness for less weakness?

emotional wounds are much harder to heal
than physical wounds
because it's hard to heal
what you cannot see
and many times
we don't even realize they are there

i can't just take a pill twice a day
for four weeks
to heal the childhood trauma i grew up with

yes, physical wounds damage us immensely,
but emotional ones are even more harmful
because they keep bleeding
long after we've stopped noticing the pain

nobody ever supported me.
if people just listened to me, everything would be fine.
somehow, every ex i've had was crazy.

magically,
you were flawless
yet every time you complained
about the people around you,
only one name kept showing up

so tell me,
if you have a problem with everyone you meet,
does that tell me more about them?
or does that tell me more about you?

love still has its hands around my throat
even after your departure,
your presence still bounces around in my thoughts,
still presents itself in my actions,
and refuses to leave no matter how hard i beg it to

i'm always exhausted
yet cannot sleep

i'm always hungry
yet cannot eat

i'm always anxious
yet cannot think

i know that i'm slowly breaking inside,
that peace is farther and farther away
as the hours turn to days
and the days turn to weeks,
but i can't seem to stop crumbling

i'm a flame that begs to be hugged by wind,
knowing it will blow me out
as soon as it touches me

there's no point in leaving,
because even if i ran to the ends of the earth,
i know you'd be waiting for me there

YOU'RE SO SENSITIVE YOU'RE SO SENSITIVE YOU'RE SO SENSITIVE YOU'RE SO SENSITIVE (*but it did hurt, so why doesn't that matter to you?*)

I KNOW WHAT'S BEST FOR YOU I KNOW WHAT'S BEST FOR YOU I KNOW WHAT'S BEST FOR YOU I KNOW WHAT'S BEST FOR YOU (*funny how you already know my life's blueprint when you never asked me for the instructions.*)

YOU'RE THE REASON I'M LIKE THIS YOU'RE THE REASON I'M LIKE THIS YOU'RE THE REASON I'M LIKE THIS (*but i'm not the one hurting you... you're hurting me.*)

YOU RUIN EVERYTHING YOU RUIN EVERYTHING YOU RUIN EVERYTHING YOU RUIN EVERYTHING (*if i ruin everything, then why are you still here? is it because you need something to ruin?*)

NO ONE ELSE WOULD LOVE YOU IF THEY REALLY KNEW YOU NO ONE ELSE WOULD LOVE YOU IF THEY REALLY KNEW YOU NO ONE ELSE WOULD LOVE YOU IF THEY REALLY KNEW YOU (*do you know the real me? do i know the real me?*)

YOU'RE THE TOXIC ONE YOU'RE THE TOXIC ONE YOU'RE THE TOXIC ONE YOU'RE THE TOXIC ONE (*i'm not toxic. you are. no, maybe i'm just overreacting. or am i? maybe i am just like you...*)

I HATE YOU I HATE YOU I HATE YOU (*i hate me too. maybe that's the only thing we ever agreed on.*)

it feels like i'm always on trial for your love
i'm the one who plans the dates
i'm the one who shows affection first
i'm the one who gives without receiving anything in return

it's not that i expect something back when i give,
but is it too much to ask
for a little love
in return for all the late-night check ins
and soft morning kisses i gave you?

it's like i'm SHOUTING into a canyon

but the wind
swallows my words
before they can reach you

i am heard,
but never reached

i just don't get it.

we did everything together
and planned the rest of our lives with each other,
so how did we go from *always* to *almost*?
i mean, everything used to be so clear.
you gave me certainty in the way you always texted goodnight,
in the way you stayed up late just to listen to what i had to say,
in being the only place in this world where i actually felt *safe*.

but one day, everything began to change.
we stopped shering little moments together.
arguments became a part of our dailee routine.
i felt like a strangur in my own home,
like i was speaking a foren language.

yuo sed it wsa nothng, but it flt lke evryhting.
it awl flet two lowd and to quite.
too fst nd two slwo.
to mcuh nd knot enouf.
t'is lke soemtingh crakd nside f em taht i c'atn ptu bak tgethre.
i dno't no wath's reel, jsut waht herts.

i droun't kauv w'hu iym wh'thoox yuhru.
hau kanth sm'rrynx feolh s'reel n'styll f'lth aparnth?
dyjoo evrulv meh'dh weh the luhvnd jyu?
hurr'du iynluv suhmwuhn whoux stilth felx laikh hou'muh?
itz narthe ennduv th'whrrl'd, b't ish'r feylx lyyk et.

i just don't get it.

i endured every cruel word,
slammed door,
and raised hand,
because i kept telling myself
that it would be okay in the end,
that we'd outlast the storms,
but i didn't know "the end"
meant our end
i didn't leave
because i assumed you wouldn't either

i wasted years building a boat with rotting wood,
breathing in decay, though i swore it smelled good
ignoring the creaks as the damage spread,
until it sank, and i wished i had fled

from you, to you

what you say:

you're always
too sensitive

stop it, you're
overreacting

why do you always
make everything
so difficult?

you can't do
anything right

you need me
more than i need you

what i hear:

my feelings
don't matter to you

your pain is
inconvenient to me

am i the reason
nothing feels easy?

maybe i was never
meant to succeed
at anything

am i truly nothing
without you?

we used to orbit each other
two stars in the same constellation
always close enough to shine together

even lightyears away,
you felt within reach
gravity kept our hearts aligned
and the pull between us kept us grounded
but eventually, you began to float away
you were near enough to see,
yet too far to *feel*

now, you feel galaxies away
despite being in the same room as me,
a star i can sense and see
but cannot touch

how can a galaxy
filled with shining stars
feel so much like an empty sky?

i wish i didn't notice the way you stopped caring

how your *good-morning* essays
turned into one-word replies

how your spontaneous kisses
turned into casual hugs

how your continuous compliments
turned into constant criticisms

i wish i didn't notice the way you stopped caring
because maybe then,
i'd have stopped caring too

when i gave you my heart, it was fragile and delicate
it was formed through trauma and sorrow
that i carried throughout my childhood

you were supposed to take care of it
you were supposed to comfort it
and help heal it

instead,
you took advantage of it
abused it
and restricted its growth

my heart now lies in fragments across the floor,
every shard a symbol of what once shined
each attempt to mend deepens the fracture inside me
yet i keep gathering fragments
hoping one day they'll align again

marriage isn't easy,
because when love is tested,
the choice is simple
but never easy:
either hold on tighter
or let go for good

too many vows dissolve into divorce
though all begin with hope
for lifelong love

i always questioned why people put themselves in positions
to choose between love and pain
yet here i am
doing the same

right person, wrong time?
no.

wrong person, right time?
no.

wrong time, wrong person?
mhm.
and i stayed anyway.

i have developed a fear of falling in love again.
a terror rooted not in love or romance, but in survival.
this fear is not something i was born with.
it was forcibly given to me,
shaped over time by someone who supposedly loved me.

the fear began as love, or at least, was disguised as love.
but cruelty quietly crept in.
i was trapped in the grips of control and manipulation.
i began to question myself,
shrinking as fear invaded every space love once held.

the eggshells beneath me shattered with every step,
yet there was no other path for me to choose.
i winced at the sound of a raised voice
and cringed after every sudden blow.
i scanned every single room i entered and mapped every exit,
yet stayed in place. my body reacted before my mind could.
i flinched after every slammed door and every raised hand.
the only peace i found was when i was alone,
but even then,
it flickered out too soon.

their behavior didn't just make me fear them.
it made me fear myself.
i didn't know what to believe.
i began to confuse right from wrong,
and ignored the red flags that kept blinding my vision.
loving them meant unlearning how to love myself,
but it was a price i was forced to pay,
because my fear of them overcame the love i had for myself.
i once feared loneliness.
now, i fear love, and wonder how to live without loneliness.

hard times are supposed to make you stronger
but they only made me weaker

i'm not even sure how i survived
because i barely had the strength
to peel my head from the pillow
before all this happened

i'm grateful that the storm is over
but it washed away the foundation
i needed to stand again

i may be a survivor,
but i feel more like a shadow,
a remnant of the light i used to carry

i used to feel *whole*,
but now i'm just a collection of pieces
that don't fit together

i don't know *how* i became
someone i don't recognize
yet here i am,
a mere outline
of the person i once was

i'm in between cutting you off entirely
and giving you one final chance
because when your name flashes across my screen,
half of me wants to answer
and half of me wants to run

i will not forget anything you did,
because despite all the pain you caused me,
there is still space in my heart for forgiveness
but that doesn't mean i'm not scared

i know that getting close to you could destroy me,
and as much as i'm willing to put my trust in you again,
my heart cannot carry any more pain

it's not that i'm moving on,
but i'm not holding on either
i don't know how to live without you,
but i don't know how i can possibly survive with you

both choices feel wrong
and maybe there is no *right* one

the beginning of our love was electrifying
you made me feel seen, unique, alive,
like love was worth fighting for

but then the warning signs started appearing
your temper in some moments,
your silence in others,
made me feel smaller than i already felt

more red flags appeared,
yet my love for you placed a blindfold over me
and i did not even notice them
my heart whispered warnings,
but i silenced it
and told it to stop being overdramatic

before i knew it,
i was in the midst of chaos,
unsure how i got there,
blind to the wreckage around me
the love that once rescued me
became the weight that drowned me
i was in the eye of the storm,
at a standstill
as destruction whirled around me

i don't regret loving you
because for a moment,
what we shared was beautiful

but i regret not leaving you sooner,
because once the mask fell,
the storm made landfall

icouldnotbemyselfaroundyoubecauseyouwould getmad. youstartedrestrictingmyemotionssayi- ngiwastoosensitiveandnoteverythinghadtobea bigdeal. youmademesecond-guessmyselfandit turnedintocontrollingbehavior. *youshouldn'tw- earthat.it'sembarrassingwhenyoulaughtooloud. peopledon'tlikeyouwhenyoutalktoomuch.* the morecontrolyougained,themoresilenceattain- ed. yousaidishouldsmilemorebutonlywhenthe timewasright. yousaidbeingquietwasbetterthan beingwrong. yousaidineededtostopseeingmyfr- iends. everythingaboutme-myvoicemyattitude myactions-waseither*toomuch*or*notenough.* iw- asreshapedbyyouandicouldnotmovewithoutyo- urapproval.iwasconfinedtotheboxyouputmein.

i didn't deserve the way you treated me
i didn't deserve to lose lifelong friends
i didn't deserve to apologize for things i never did
i didn't deserve to be insulted every single day
i didn't deserve to feel like i would never be enough
i didn't deserve to feel guilty for being *me*

if this is love,
then love needs a new name

no human being should ever be made
to feel this small,
let alone the person you claim you love
you treated me as if i was the worst person
to have ever entered your life
but i was just a broken soul
giving you the love i was searching for too

the last time you hit me, you said,
it hurts me more than it hurts you
that i'd never understand how much it broke your heart,
but you already forgot what you did
while it replays in a loop in my mind every single day

you act as if you didn't have the power
to stop,
but it was always in your hands

some of the scars you left will eventually fade,
but most of them were never meant to heal

anxiety is a deafening entity that has built a nest in my soul.
it ricochets through my mind,
it screams inside my chest,
and it is relentlessly dismantling my peace.
and yet,
on the outside,
everything appears calm and pleasant.
it is a siren blaring in a soundproof room,
but it is only soundproof to the people around me.

as much as i try to suppress it,
anxiety always finds a way to be seen.
it holds races in my mind,
forcing thoughts to overlap and repeat.
it creates a drumline that travels from my heart to my ears.
it produces a dizzying spin throughout my body,
places boulders inside my throat,
and forms oceans beneath my eyes.
it demands release.
but it never leaves.

and yet,
on the outside,
i look perfectly fine.
the people around me see someone who always smiles
and says *i'm fine*.
they see someone 'normal',
but inside is anything *but* normal.

there's a disconnect between the outside and the inside,
and it makes everything heavier.
i'm drowning invisibly and i want people to notice,
but at the same time,
i feel ashamed for feeling this way.
i'm the one who always helps the people around me,
yet i struggle to ask for help myself.

then again,
it's hard to ask for help
when you look like you don't need it.

you'd think time would give me control over my anxiety,
but if anything,
it's gotten worse.
the siren that blared around me
is now an alarm that is present 24/7,
and the worst part is,
it's become white noise.

for someone who's always hated storms,
i've learned to live inside one.

you placed me at a crossroads
where i must choose between two roads
each one reeking of smoke and rust,
as if both paths have already burned

one is paved with broken glass
and haunted by screams
the other dissolves into fog
with every step i take

neither gets me closer to home;
both lead me away from who i used to be

every bridge i build c
               o
               l
                l
                a
               p
                s
                 e
                s
                    underneath me

every door i open
  [locks]
    [locks]
  [locks]
behind me

every finish line i approach
      sprints further-
              the closer-
                       i arrive.

my therapist said,
there's always a rainbow after every storm.
but what if the storms never end?
what if the wreckage makes rainbows as useless
as paper towels in a flood?
i want to believe in them,
even when i know better,
but as soon as i take in their majesty,
their glow fades under the thunder of the next storm.

it feels like i'm here,
but not really here
i exist physically,
but i am absent emotionally

the agony you wrapped around my heart
numbed all i used to feel
and shut down the rest of me

i move,
but only as someone else's shadow
i don't feel real anymore–
just a silhouette of who i used to be

it's like i'm looking at a complete stranger,
but at the same time,
a lesser version of myself

i survived.
but was it myself i sacrificed?

ii.

i wasn't a person to you. i was just a project, something to keep you busy when life grew dull. you reduced me to a lifeless thing in your hands, not a human being with feelings. i hid the *real* me (and you never noticed), but it was a debt paid in neglect, as i couldn't even tell who i was anymore.

your approach made me feel incomplete, as if i was always in need of repair. i didn't need constant criticism, countless comparisons, or crippling confinement. i needed understanding. i needed acceptance. i needed love. your obsession over "fixing" me was never about repair. it was always about control.

at first, i believed in your illusion of repair. i thought you cared, thought you wanted to help. but then, the cracks started forming. every attempt at fixing me erased another piece of myself. you reshaped parts of me that never needed changing. i felt myself becoming undone, and your attempt to fix me left me more broken than ever before.

you never asked how i felt. you stripped away the little self-worth i had left. you made me question my own judgment and believe there was something flawed about me. you made me feel like a failure and ashamed to be myself. my heart was fragile enough without you, and every adjustment left more unseen scars. i'm not made of parts to be rearranged. i'm made of feelings to be honored.

i should never have been a project. i should never have let you work on me as you pleased. i was whole in so many other ways than you understood. you made me lose trust in the people around me, lose faith in the One above me, and lose confidence in the one within me. you took a lot from me, and destroyed parts of me you had no right to touch. and yet i'm still here. i have not disappeared. i will gather all the parts of me you could not take, the parts of me that refused to break, and rebuild them into someone who will no longer ache.

if you're traveling with someone who needs help,
secure your own oxygen mask before assisting them.
i saw that message on my feed the other day,
and it stuck with me
like fingerprints across my heart

for too long,
i tore holes in my own lungs
just to fill yours with air,
a mistake that left me gasping,
one i won't repeat

because if i have to reduce *my* breath
just to give *you* life,
am i really living?
or am i just breathing lifeless air?

i was fading away,
drowning in an ocean of misery,
but hope grabbed me
and pulled me toward the surface

abuse didn't end me,
though at times i wished it had,
hope traced my scars
as proof i was *alive*

you spent years drowning me
in anger disguised as love,
but it taught me the difference
between love behind a mask
and love that showed its face

you taught me lessons,
some sharper than others,
but the greatest lesson you gave me
was to see love revealed as forgiveness
and when i forgave you,
i learned to love myself again

to the ones who left too soon

i.

joy was a droplet of water
in the desert that was my soul
grief invaded me
and extracted the last trickle i had left

i felt violated,
too drained to resist
and now,
absence haunts the spaces joy once filled

a stranger:
hello
goodbye

the space between us was only a breath, but it was still memorable

a friend:
hello

goodbye

the space between us spanned an entire childhood, and though life pulled us apart, it was still wonderful

you:
hello

goodbye

the space between us spanned a lifetime, but it still didn't feel like enough time to find the right goodbye.

grief is a thief
that carried you from this world
and stripped my joy from me

i just wanted my light back,
but if i'd gotten my wish,
grief would never have found you

my mind is an ocean filled with drifting m e m o r i e s.

the way
you made my
favorite meal,
just for me

the way you
laughed at your
own jokes

the way you walked
to water the
garden

the way you played old
board games at
the kitchen table

the way your
perfume
lingered in
the air

the way you
always swore
your family stories
were true

the way i always
felt small and at peace
in your arms no matter how
old i grew

these memories have no place to go
they're just drifting at sea,
begging to be noticed,
just to exist again

at first,
the pain was piercing
as i tried to accept
the truth that you left too soon
i was trapped in a cycle of sadness
with no escape

my only escape was sleep,
but even dreams became nightmares
that lingered when i woke

at this moment,
pain no longer overtakes me,
i've grown numb to it
exhaustion has taken its place,
as i am too tired to even respond
to everyone who asks if i'm okay

it doesn't even hurt anymore
i am utterly exhausted

Tony Cardona

many pet owners hate the sound
of their dog barking at absolutely nothing,
until the silence of their departure
is louder than any bark

many parents hate the sight
of the mess their children leave everywhere,
until every room is spotless
because they are all completely empty

many children hate the way
their parents call the phone so often,
until they scroll through old voicemails
just to hear the sound of their voice

and many people hate the feeling
of never having any alone time,
until the only sound left
is the echo of their thoughts

we don't appreciate what we have
until it slips away
and loneliness becomes a mirror
we cannot look away from

heartache would weigh less heavily
if i could remove the daily reminders
of what once belonged to us

i am aware of my surroundings much more than i was before
i notice the empty chair at the dining room table,
the one that always creaked but never broke,
the absence of the distinct sound your footprints made
when you walked down the stairs,
the shortage of *dings* accompanied by your name
lighting up my phone

i now dread the days i once loved
christmases feel muted,
birthdays hollow,
anniversaries unbearable,
your absence is louder now
than your presence ever was

i'm torn between remembering and forgetting
because if i removed everything
that reminded me of you,
i wouldn't have to carry the weight of longing

but to forget the pain,
i'd have to forget the chair that creaked,
the stairs that echoed,
the dings that once sang your name,

i'd have to forget you.

one of the things
that hurts me the most
is i didn't properly say goodbye

i feel like i should have *done* more
like i should have *said* more
to keep us from breaking
but then again
what *is* the right way to say goodbye?

it's not something that can be taught
it's something that has to be stumbled through

i could spend a lifetime
learning how to say goodbye
and i still wouldn't know
how

it's hard to let go of you
when you created a home inside my heart
in the shape of your soul

you gave my heart rest
after years of weariness
but now,
it feels like a stranger
in its own home

i left the door to my heart unlocked
knowing you won't come back,
but secretly hoping that one day
you'll walk back in

i didn't realize how destructive grief was
until it became my only companion

i understood that everyone experiences grief
but to be honest,
i didn't expect it to come so quickly

i found it easy to console others
with words

yet it was impossible
to do the same
for myself

the advice i gave others
never reached me
and i was clueless
about grief
about
me

i was not ready to say goodbye because i thought we'd have more time. i'd give anything to have one last conversation with you as

it feels strange to see your name on my phone
but not be able to talk to you

i saved all of your voicemails
just so i could listen to them
and pretend you're still talking to me
on the days i miss you the most

i haven't deleted our old conversations
as they are treasures i cannot let go

i didn't realize how precious the simple things were
like random texts
or quick calls
that lasted mere minutes
but stayed with me for a lifetime

i feel guilty
for the times i didn't make the time
to ask how you were

i would give anything
to hear you say

i'm good!
how about you?

one
final
time.

healing is complicated

when i first began my healing process,
i didn't know it would hurt more than the wound

i expected to feel relief,
but if anything, i feel resentment
because grief refuses to age,
always finding a way back in

grief sneaks in
when i wake up and believe you're still here,
only for a split second

grief hides in the fabric
of a shirt you hadn't worn in years
but will never wear again

grief shows up uninvited
every year on your birthday
a day meant for celebration
turned into desolation
because you are not here to celebrate with me

grief is not as constant right now
as it was in the beginning,
but i wonder
is it numbness?
or does grief simply wait
for my lowest hour?

even though years have passed since you left this world,
grief ambushes me
when i feel the same betrayal
the same anger
as the day
you were laid to rest

healing is complicated
because while most wounds heal
healing itself is essentially endless

remember when we were at a family dinner,
locked eyes,
and burst out laughing?
everyone around us looked at us as if we were insane
and that made us laugh even more.
i'll never forget the way your eyes crinkled,
the way my belly ached,
and the joy my heart felt in that moment.
the funny thing is,
the joke we were laughing about wasn't even that funny.
it was about a dog wh-

what about the time we took a road trip to tennessee?
we packed our car to the brim,
with the smell of burgers in one corner
and fresh sunscreen in another,
all while blasting our country playlist
through half-broken speakers.
we focused so much on singing songs
we didn't know the lyrics to
that we missed our exit,
and were actually headed toward ohio.
we stopped by a gas station to take a quick nap,
but were scared off by hobos.
we re-routed back toward tennessee,
and when we entered the smoky mountains,
we were hit with the most breathtaking view.
mountains towered above us and cows grazed around us.
but the most beautiful part of the view
was that the grass looked li-

i'll never forget the day we held our first picnic in chicago.
we spent the entire week planning for perfect weather,
but the day was anything but.
cold wind blew off the lake,
sea gulls shrieked above us,
and napkins took flight.
the grass was lumpy,
the fruit got warm,
and our drinks kept tipping over.
birds,
traffic,
and the L surrounded us
so we couldn't even hear each other.
and yet,
it was the most beautiful picnic i've ever had.
no matter how soggy the sandwiches
or how chaotic the city,
it was special because i got to share it with you.
as we finished the last bites of our squishy sandwiches,
the sun set into a mural just for us.
i looked over at you,
reached for your hand,
and leaned in to-

even when we did nothing at all, it was still special,
because it was with you.
but now,
you've left me
with stories
i can't finish.

if time changes everything,
why am i still waiting for change?
i thought grief would lighten with time,
but it presses down with the same weight as day one

i'm still waiting for the part
where grief sinks into background noise,
but years have passed,
and still,
nothing has changed
time moved on,
but forgot to take the pain with it

does time truly heal?

or does it just bury
what will always remain?

your toothbrush is still in the cup,
but the sink hasn't felt its movement
in...   .

i graduated   month,
and   i looked for your face in   crowd,
i remembered you   no longer   .

we   ordered extra fries to share,
but   there's   .

your favorite song   on the radio   day,
but silence sang louder than   .

i   yelled at you when you left   lights on,
but now the lights   .

you used to   steal the covers,
but last night i   enveloped by warmth
yet emptier than   .

your absence lingers everywhere
and i don't know how to fill in the gaps.

how am i supposed to move on
when i stitched pieces of myself into you–
the shirts you always borrowed,
our laughter at midnight,
the playlists i made–
and you took them with you?

perhaps it was my fault
for pouring too much of me into you,
but i didn't expect you to leave so soon,
i didn't expect the journey of finding myself again
to be this painful

will i ever truly feel like *me* again?
or is this the shadow
that will follow me
the rest of my life?

i'm the leading role
in a play i never signed up for

i'm tired of pretending everything is okay
every day, i put on a show,
acting as if everything is fine,
and the audience believes it

on the outside,
i stand beneath the stage lights,
appearing perfectly fine,
and sometimes even happy

but on the inside,
i am quickly unraveling backstage,
melting beneath the spotlight
that exposes everything i hide

i smile and laugh
to hide the sadness forming in me
i avoid eye contact
so people don't see my spotlight flicker out

sometimes,
i just want to *feel sad*
without anyone asking how i'm doing
and cry until my pillows become sponges
and scream until my vocal chords thin out
and collapse until my bones become dust
but
I
JUST
CAN'T.

because the world keeps spinning
there is no intermission
life goes on
and the next act is already waiting

even though my world stopped,
no one else did with me
so i am forced to move on
even when every part of me begs me
to hold on a little longer...

but anyway,
sorry for interrupting

the curtain is rising

it's showtime again.

i wish i had known
the last conversation we shared,
arguing over who made the better pancakes,
would be the last conversation we shared

i wish i had known
the last time you said *i love you*,
like a secret meant only for me,
would be the last time you said *i love you*

i wish i had known
the last time i hugged you,
your hoodie still smelling like the detergent you always used,
would be the last time i hugged you

i wish i had known
the last time i picked up the phone for you,
you promising you'd call me again tomorrow,
would be the last time i picked up the phone for you

i wish i had known
the last time i saw you,
your smile flashing across your face like a spark,
would be the last time i saw you

had i known,
i would have cherished every last moment
as if it were the only thing i was meant to do in life
because right now,
that's exactly what it feels like

you taught me to appreciate the simple things in life
like the smell of coffee drifting through the house,
the sound of rain tapping against the window,
and hugs that say more than words

but ever since you left me behind,
the only thing i appreciate
is silence
because it's the one thing
that understands how much i miss you

i received a call last night, and it felt like hearing sunshine
through the phone. the nurse said your health was improving,
and you'd be discharged soon.
i was relieved the storm was finally over, and i'd see you
outside white walls again.
that night, you came home.
i told you to rest, because tomorrow i wanted to spend the
whole day doing all your favorite things.

when the sun rose, that's exactly what we did.
at your favorite park, we fed the birds,
but they chased us away.
at your favorite restaurant, you ordered your usual:
a burger with no lettuce, tomatoes, cheese, onions, or mayo,
just the way you liked it.
we ended at the beach, watching the sky burn with color
as the sun kissed the ocean.

that night, i hugged you goodbye.
i said, *i'm so glad you're here.*
i love you, and i can't wait to see you tomorrow.
you held me tight and wouldn't let go, so i stayed.
but when i pulled away, everything changed.
you opened your mouth but no sound came.
the walls stretched taller, bending like rubber.
the floor rippled like water beneath me.
every blink pushed you farther. and then—
your body flickered, like a film reel skipping frames.
the world blurred, and before i knew it,
the curtains lifted from my eyes.
you weren't really back.
it was only a dream,
and once again,
i woke to a sadness that wouldn't leave.

my therapist said,
moving on doesn't mean letting go,
but what if i don't want to move on?
what if holding on is the only thing keeping me stable?
what if holding on
looks like scrolling through your old messages at 2 a.m.?
the only way to move on from you is to let you go,
but letting you go
would mean letting me go.

you may be the only one missing
but it still feels as if the entire world is empty
and it's excruciating to see people chasing promotions,
people chasing birthdays,
when i can't even take a step

my life

before you
- mornings were filled
  with excitement
  for a new day

- laughter reverberated
  throughout the house

- holidays were
  countdowns
  to excitement

- i smiled often
  without even noticing

- the world was vibrant
  and full of color

- my heart was grounded
  in what it was

- the future was a dream
  we both shared
  and looked forward to

after you
- mornings are heavy
  reminders of my days
  starting without you

- silence settles
  over the dust of
  untouched photographs

- holidays are
  ticking time bombs
  of memories past

- i have forgotten
  how to smile
  without forcing it

- the world is dull
  and faded, a portrait
  stripped of color

- my heart is just floating
  around, looking for
  a place to land

- the future is
  an unfamiliar path
  i now walk alone

the day you disappeared from my life,
your absence was a reality i could not escape
mornings,
nights,
nothing feels like mine anymore

i have had to learn how to live again
slowly,
painfully,
alone,
though i was never good at living
even when you were beside me

from you, to you

what you say: what i hear:

my therapist said,
it's okay to not be okay,
but what if i'm not okay with just being okay?
what if i'm tired of not being okay?
what if i've blurred the line between forcing a smile
and actually meaning it?
what if i have confused the two so much
that i can't tell the difference
between what's okay and what's not okay?

the hardest part of it all
is shouting your name into empty rooms
hoping to hear you say mine back,
knowing i won't hear your voice,
yet breaking anyway
when i am greeted by the echo of absence

you may be in a better place,
but selfishly, i admit
i wish you were still *here*
because *my* better place
was anywhere your voice lived

how am i supposed to move on in life
when you are both everywhere
and nowhere
all at once?
i see you in everything
yet never in front of me

i am grateful
for the beautiful reminders you left behind,
like the songs you used to play in the kitchen,
or the birthday cards you never forgot to write,
but those reminders sting as much as they soothe
because they breathe life into wounds
i've long fought to let fade away

ii.

"Fatal Car Crash Claims the Lives of Two Teens"

**"Family Devastated
After House Fire Leaves Them Homeless"**

**"Police Investigate Homicide
After Body Found Near River"**

when we read headlines,
we are naturally inclined
to see them as mere numbers,
but they are more than just statistics
they are new realities
for lives forever changed

when someone passes away in a car crash,
there isn't just one life affected
a mother lost her son
a teacher lost her student
a sibling lost his only friend

my perspective on tragedy has shifted
from looking at statistics as just mere numbers
to looking at them as new realities
and it's taught me to meet loss
with compassion

nothing could erase what we shared

i will never forget
our late-night talks,
where vulnerability reached the deepest parts of us

i will never forget
our celebrations,
like watching the same movie again and again
and loving it every time

i will never forget
your support,
a comfort i had never known before,
one that quieted my anxiety

though you may no longer be here,
you are always present
in the countless memories you left for me

you may have left *this* world
but you will never leave *my* world

i'm still searching for the closure i never got
i can't help but look for it everywhere
even in the places i've already searched

i wish the answers to my *whys* could find me
so i can finally move on

why so soon?
why couldn't i stop it?

why didn't i call more often?
why did i take our time for granted?

how could God let this happen?
why is life so unfair?

why does it always have to be me?
and yet, the answers never come

but maybe that's the thing
maybe i am struggling to find closure
because some things aren't meant to have an ending

maybe,
just maybe,
the only way to find true closure
is to stop looking for it
where it isn't meant to be
and learn to live without it

for years, i carried anger toward grief
until someone shared words that softened me:
grief is just love with nowhere to go
and i began to see it with sympathy

the reason grief is felt so much
is the presence of the love that preceded it
the more love there was,
the more grief will be felt

when love has no place to rest,
it reshapes into grief
that does not know where to turn,
what to do,
who to choose,
so it does the only thing it knows:
inflict pain

when i put my arm around grief
and comforted it during its lonely moments,
something inside us shifted
love started peeking in again
and slowly returned to me

although there are still days
when grief swells larger than i can hold,
i am learning to sit beside it
to remind it that it is still worthy of love
just as much of every one of us

grief is simply the price we pay for love

love is a connection that runs so deep,
the only way to capture its magnificence
is to experience it yourself
genuine love is more valuable
than the moments time has stolen
it is more precious
than the memories carved into our bones
it is the one force
that transcends any and all evil

as for grief,
it is heavy
it is painful
it comes and goes in unexpected waves
it is the shadow love leaves behind
and i wish it didn't exist
but if it didn't exist,
perhaps love wouldn't be as valuable as it is

if i had to choose between loving you
but experiencing grief,
or avoiding grief
at the cost of losing love for you,
i would welcome grief
with open arms

grief is love's way of holding on,
even when everything else has let go,
like a voice that still echoes after the room is empty

the connection between grief and love
isn't sorrow's punishment,
but memory's gift,
proof that love endures
even when all else fades

i will not let what we shared
disappear with you
i will continue to tell our story,
not just in the words i speak,
but in the way i live

while your memory may dwindle,
and your photographs may fade,
your meaning never will
it is the truth that time cannot erase

you weren't just someone i loved
you were someone who *changed* me
your love,
your kindness,
your compassion for others
shaped me into someone i can finally be proud of

from this day forward,
i will live my life in a way
that keeps you alive in spirit
i want to leave a mark on others
the way you left one on me,
through gentleness,
through affection,
and by simply choosing to love

your departure isn't the end of your story
it is a continuation of it
though your absence is real,
your love endures,
proof that nothing,
not even death,
can silence love

you may no longer be present,
but you will never stop being felt in the present

you are present
when the streetlight flickers
at the corner you always stopped to wait for me

you are present
when the same cardinal visits me every morning
to hum a lullaby that reaches my soul

you are present
when certain dreams about you feel *different*
calm, vivid, and comforting

you may no longer be *here*,
but you will always be near

i kept trying to fill your void
with borrowed smiles,
but i was always unsuccessful

i tried to stay busy
by doing laundry at midnight
and errands that didn't need doing
in an attempt to outrun grief,
but it always caught up with me

i tried to recreate you
by forcing relationships with people
who looked and acted like you,
but i was only creating an unreal connection
as imitations only highlight what's missing

i tried to replicate your legacy
by writing with your pen,
but your ink never moved the same way,
as legacy driven by desperation only leads to destruction

it took all these failures to see
that your space isn't meant to be filled or replaced
by *anything*
it is a wonderful reminder
of the light you left to guide me
and that reminder glows with its own quiet beauty

Tony Cardona

i healed much faster
when i stopped carrying your memory
as a winter coat i wore through every season,
and traded it for open air woven with kindness,
soft enough to let me breathe again

you may be gone,
but you haven't stopped teaching me life lessons

i sense your patience in the red lights
that remind me to breathe before moving forward

i feel your love when i water the plants
and watch them lean toward light

i hear your pride in the scratch of a pen
as i sign my name on what i've built

though i may feel lonely,
you have taught me
that i am never really alone
and even emptiness carries your presence

i used to avoid our old memories,
as they only hurt me.
the melodies of songs,
the smell of foods,
the sight of photos—
each carried an overwhelming wave of sadness,
and the only way to protect myself was to avoid them.

but avoidance quickly turned into emptiness.
pushing away our moments,
i began forgetting them,
like losing you all over again.
forgetting you felt lonelier than grief.

so i let the memories creep back in.
i listened to our songs,
ate our meals,
looked at our pictures again.
though bittersweet,
each memory sparked a flicker of warmth in my soul,
a closeness i'd been pushing away.

imagine how lonely i would feel
if i let our memories go with you.
but i haven't.
instead, i hold them close.
memories don't remind me you're gone.
they show me how you live on.

the world around me feels eerily silent,
like a stage after the curtain falls,
but every once in a while,
if i stop and listen closely enough,
i can hear your voice beneath it all,
a softness that steadies the spiral in me,
wrapping me in three simple lines:
"i'm okay.
you're okay.
everything will be okay."

when you left this world,
you weren't just absent
you were nonexistent
for the first time in my life,
i missed something more than i loved it

but my longing for you deepened our love
the ache in my heart made space
for tenderness to take root
yearning didn't diminish love
it proved the depths of love's endurance
it turned graves into gardens

but it wasn't all joyful
while missing you led to loving you more,
loving you led to missing you even more,
and it created an endless tide my heart was caught in,
pulled back and forth without rest
the lines between the two blurred into each other,
until i couldn't tell the difference
between loving you
and missing you

my heart's evolution
ended in me holding love and longing simultaneously
melancholy and joy existed in the same space
and became partners as opposed to adversaries

for every cold breeze,
there was a gust of warmth
for every storm,
there was a surge of tranquility
for every tear,
there was a smile waiting to meet it

i didn't have to find a cure for my longing
i just had to find meaning in it

your absence feels like a tide inside my chest,
never strong enough to drown me,
but always pulling me under
i don't just feel *sad*
i can literally feel my heart breaking apart within me

though some time has passed since your departure,
my heart is still punctured
with a hole in the shape of your name,
a crater of scar tissue
that will forever be present

time has helped a little,
but it does more patching than healing
it is a flat tire that's been repaired,
but no longer trustworthy
it is a blemish covered with makeup,
but always visible to me
it is a leaking dam covered with duct tape,
a futile attempt at hiding a barrage
that will inevitably come

they say the seasons turn,
and *it gets better*,
but if that's the case,
why does winter still linger in me?

i mean,
the pain may not define me,
but it lives within me
love and pain coexist in a strange way,
where the deeper the love,
the more permanent the wound

but maybe that isn't such a bad thing
maybe some wounds refuse to heal
because healing now
would mean erasing the love that carried me here

the bond we shared was too bright
to be dimmed by absence

for even at night,
the moon still borrows the sun's light
to glow in the sky

even in the dark,
one candle is enough
to guide your next steps

and even shadows themselves
depend on light
to exist in the first place

though darkness may linger,
even the longest nights bend toward morning

"hey. don't cry. it's okay. i'm still here. you may not see me, but that doesn't mean i'm not here with you. i know you feel sad and lonely, but i want you to know i'm still with you, just in different ways.

"i sent a cardinal the other day, and she told me you looked beautiful. did you notice the flower i planted, out of season just for you? i played our song on the radio, the one you never knew the words to but always sang anyway. sometimes i even visit your dreams, so you know how close i still am.

"i'm sorry i had to leave so soon, but i was needed up here. i didn't abandon you. God knew you needed comfort in a different way. i can watch over you here more than i ever could there.

"don't be sad. i may seem far, but the love we shared keeps us close. love doesn't end with goodbye. it just lives differently.

"i'm proud of who you've become. you've shown strength in the face of everything that tried to break you. you're growing into your best self, even if you don't see it yet. hang in there for me. you'll never be alone because i'll always be by your side. i haven't gone far. i've just gone ahead. you're amazing. don't forget that."

to the one who chose to stay

today, i choose to let go

i choose to let go of conditional love
i am not a backup plan
i am someone worth showing up for
i will no longer fight to stay in places
where i'm only welcome when i'm useful

i choose to let go of self-blame
it is not my job
to take responsibility for other people's wounds
i no longer carry shame
that does not belong to me

i choose to let go of what could have been
because holding on to what *almost* was
stops me from embracing what *is*
letting go frees my hands
to hold what is actually here

i choose to let go of what weighs me down
i no longer mistake heaviness
for importance,
because peace should not be a luxury

i forgive myself
for staying too long
in places i outgrew

for a long time, i was infuriated with God and questioned everything about Him. nothing went to plan. people walked away or were taken from my life. suffering was relentless, joy nonexistent. i lived in a fog of confusion and disappointment, asking why God would pour so much pain into someone He claimed to love.

but despite everything telling me not to, i slowly began to put my faith in Him. it wasn't overnight, but a gradual loosening of my grip. i started to believe there might be a greater reason behind my struggles, even if i couldn't see it yet. i planted seeds of faith in silence and let my tears water them.

the more i trusted Him, the more He revealed. He removed people who held me back from becoming who i was meant to be. pain wasn't punishment; it was preparation. through suffering, i was shaped and refined, like metal in fire. the joys He withheld were not rejection, but protection, because He knew they could lead to my downfall.

i am who i am because of what i endured. my pain will not define me because God holds that authority. the moment i surrendered was the moment i received the peace i'd prayed for for years. all He wanted was my trust. once i gave Him my faith, He did what i could never do alone. His plan was never about control. it was always about freedom. freedom born from trust in Him.

i used to be terrified of rejection
and the sadness that came along with it

it made me feel exposed,
betrayed,
and unworthy
i questioned myself
every moment of every day
but over time,
i learned to embrace rejection
and make the most of it

rejection really *is* redirection,
and all i had to do
was take a detour
that saved me from a dead end,
a road that lets me grow without apology

and now i walk steadier,
every *no* clearing space
for the *yes* meant for me

i always wondered why it was so hard
to love the people around me the way i wanted to
affection felt forced
and compassion was obscured,
but the answer to my question
was in the source all along: me

how could i expect to love them
if i didn't even love myself?
i was trying to light candles
with an unlit match
i was building bridges
with broken beams
i was incapable of loving others
because i disregarded the first step:
love
my struggle was never about them
it was about me
so i began the daily, intentional work
of renewal and inner healing

i nourished myself with kindness
like daily bread that never runs out
i replenished myself with patience,
still waters quieting my soul
i refreshed myself with forgiveness,
mercies new every morning

as i nurtured my own heart,
i was able to pour into others more
love stopped feeling prescribed
and started feeling natural

for years, i believed self-care was selfish,
but it's actually one of the most selfless things i can do
for the people around me
it is the foundation for loving others,
and places that once felt like walls
now stand as open gates of grace
where hope streams through
and i walk freely in it

the love that was restricted inside of me
now flows like rivers of living water

today, i am calmer,
gentler,
and less burdened
than yesterday

i spoke gently
instead of shouting
i took a ten-minute walk
to get some fresh air

i still ache,
but it feels quieter

tomorrow, i will be even more tranquil
and even more cheerful
than i was today

these small steps may seem insignificant now,
but they are seeds of a steadier future,
roots that will hold me firm
in the tomorrows not yet lived

the day i realized
i was no longer broken
was the day i finally exhaled
after years of holding my breath

it was the instant i walked free
from the prison i built around myself

it was the morning i discovered
the key i searched for everywhere
had always been in my hands

the day i realized
i was no longer broken
was the moment i came home
to the body i once tried to leave behind

i loosened my grip on the pieces
that no longer belonged to me

i carried blame as a shield
that disguised itself as justice,
but it only left me more exposed

i let fear creep into every decision i made,
whispering the lie
that silence was safety

i let anger consume me
and almost broke the ones
who truly cared for me

i buried blame,
fear,
and anger,

and carved space for forgiveness,
courage,
and peace

though i am still growing,
i honor my progress
and celebrate how far i've come

i   never   knew   how   to
stand   up   for   myself.   i   let
people   talk   over   me,   accepted
blame   that   wasn't   mine,   and
always   shrunk   when   faced   with
confrontation.   but   eventually,   the   silence
of   being   overlooked   grew   heavier   than
speaking   up.   now,   i   know   how   to   use
my   volume, stop apologizing for things i didn't do,
and welcome confrontation as if looking into a fearless mirror.
i'm proud of how much i've grown, because if i don't stand up
for myself, who will?

healing didn't come the way i expected
not through cinematic breakthroughs,
climactic epiphanies,
or dramatic resolutions,
but quietly,
camouflaged in ordinary moments

it came in the shuffle of my shoes on the sidewalk,
as movement quieted my mind
without needing direction

it came in the hush of rain,
as every tap against the window
represented a flower gaining life

it came in the clicks of mugs and spoons
as the warmth of coffee travelled from the cup
to my fingertips
to my soul

i couldn't see it then,
but little things added up
consistency taught me
progress doesn't need to roar
softness is powerful,
a refusal to grow bitter
despite all that tried to poison it

i didn't rush it
i didn't force it
i allowed healing to be
and it allowed me to be

(a peek into my heart)

to false love: thank you.
your absence taught me what presence really means. because
of you, i know the difference between being chosen and being
needed. you allowed me to grow stronger by teaching me that
love should never feel like a guessing game.

to loneliness: thank you.
in your silence, i started to hear things i had buried beneath
distraction. through you, i met parts of myself i had neglected
for far too long. you taught me how to prepare for love when it
came quietly.

to words that cut too deep: thank you.
the criticism behind your voice allowed me to find my own—
gentler, kinder, and stronger. from your cruelty, i learned the
power of kindness, especially in how i speak to myself. i turned
your sharpness into softness and your poison into medicine.

to betrayal: thank you.
while your dishonesty destroyed the house, it revealed that it
was built on sand. you cleared away everything i didn't need,
even if it hurt to watch it go. because of you, i found people
who welcomed me with open hands and honest hearts.

to abuse: thank you.
escaping you taught me the value of peace without explanation.
you tried to strip me of my worth, convincing me i was
unworthy of love or safety. but in the emptiness you left, i built
a foundation on gentleness. you allowed me to find
compassion, for myself, and for those still learning they
deserve to be free.

my therapist said,
healing is a journey, not a destination,
and i finally get it.
i used to be obsessed with the destination.
i thought the point was to get there as fast as i could,
rushing past sunsets,
skipping over laughter.
but one stop looked like a diner at midnight,
coffee gone cold but my friends still warm with laughter.
another exit was pulling over to watch the rain,
realizing i was allowed to rest.
i've learned it's the stops and exits along the way
that matter most,
and somewhere between them,
i arrived.

looking back,
i'm not sure if i ever felt safe in my own body

i didn't know what comfort felt like
as it had never been mine
my whole life,
i grew up in a body that felt more like a war zone
than a sanctuary
it was hard for my soul to return home
when it didn't know what *home* was in the first place

but then, safety began to bloom
in the smallest moments
i set boundaries,
introduced gentleness into my life,
and began to mend what was broken
i didn't know it at the time,
but i was slowly building a home
for my soul to rest in

the first time i felt safe in my own body was a quiet miracle
there was calm in my chest
silence no longer felt fearful
i could breathe deeply
without shrinking
and could look in the mirror
without flinching
it was an enormous exhale
after spending years holding my breath

comfort grew slowly but surely,
and i finally felt like i belonged to myself
it wasn't just one moment
it was a series of gentle moments,
a tide of calm
that softened all my instability

softly,
in the background
i finally felt safe in my own body

i finally belonged to myself

one day, i made a life-altering decision:
i started collecting all the apologies i never got.

i gathered them quietly, one by one.
apologies from the ones who never truly loved me.
apologies from the ones who only appeared when convenient.
apologies from the ones who mistook control for love.
apologies from the ones who left when i needed them most.

i stopped asking for explanations.
i stopped chasing closure.
i simply collected every unsaid *i'm sorry*
and placed them all in a pile.
then, i did what i should have done a long time ago.

i chose flames over silence.

i set them on fire.
watched them burn.
and left them in the past—where they belonged.
as i sifted through the ashes,
i found relief in knowing
that nothing worth keeping had survived.

because waiting for apologies that were never going to come
only kept me rooted in the past.
and the only person still bleeding from all those wounds
was me.

so i accepted every apology i never received
and i forgave them,
even for the times
they weren't even sorry.

part of my depression was anger i swallowed whole, trapped inside, denied a voice. not *all* my depression was anger, but much of it was a fire i refused to extinguish.

i buried anger at the people who left when i needed them, at the cruelty of the world, at the way love turned into hurt, at how things *were* instead of how they *should have been*. most of all, i was angry at how the world taught us to stay silent and slowly disappear.

over time, anger hardened into sadness, until i felt nothing. but one day, i decided to release it—not destructively, like a volcano, but gently, like a balloon releasing air. i stopped pretending and finally let the anger leave my chest and my soul.

depression didn't vanish, but it loosened its grip. as anger left, peace had space to arrive, waiting beneath everything i carried.

for too long,
my home was a garden overgrown with regret

the words i left unsaid
the time i let go to waste
the love given to those who didn't return it
the chances that came but i never took

these regrets weighed me down
and followed me everywhere i went

eventually,
i got tired of carrying the weight,
so i dug a hole within my soul
and decided to bury it all there

i proceeded to plant seeds in its place,
and each one grew,
blooming into something beautiful

they may be small,
they may be fragile,
but that doesn't take away from their beauty

growth came because i chose to let go,
and from what once buried me,
something breathtaking began to bloom

forgiveness acceptance peace compassion sympathy grace

i used to seek comfort in all the wrong places.
i searched for peace in people and places that reached for me,
but never caught me.
it wasn't that the people and places themselves
were disingenuous,
but if i didn't feel at home within myself,
how could i expect to be comfortable with others?

so i began to dust off corners,
open windows,
and make space for what was needed.
i let go of shame and slowly learned how to stay.
i was proud and grateful for how much i'd grown
by doing something as simple as coming home to myself.

i have finally become the home i spent years searching for,
the right place i never thought i'd find.
i've claimed the space of a home i no longer want to leave.
here, the walls do not close in.
they hold me.

my therapist said,
sometimes you have to break before you can heal,
and i finally get it.
seeds must crack open in soil to grow.
butterflies must break through their cocoons to fly.
freedom exists only when chains are shattered.
i had to break to begin again.
even while breaking,
i wasn't broken.
i was whole in ways i couldn't yet see.

if my heart had *before* and *after* pictures,
the differences would be remarkable.

before,

it was da-   maged, dark,
and depleted. it was   tarred and brittle,
clinging to breath   that never came. it was
cracked like old pa-   vement, overrun by weeds
that grew from neglect.   it was faded, like a ph-
otograph left in the sun   for too long, pale and
losing details. it beat   cautiously, as if it didn't
trust the world with   its rhythm. it was
heavy from carrying   memories that
no longer serv-   ed it. it was cold
from underg-   oing too many
winters it   never
asked   for.

from you, to you

after,

it is alive,   radiating,
and restored. it   is vibrant, like
stained-glass windows catching morning light.
it is soft but sturdy, like memory foam that holds
shape and supports weight. it is covered in wild-
flowers, proof that something beautiful can
still grow from ruin. it beats to celebrate
its liveliness. it is no longer afraid of
breaking because it knows how
to rebuild. it is whole bec-
ause it used its pie-
ces to learn
how to
heal.

what you say: what i hear:

i love the way   *the courage*
you've stepped   *you found looks*
into yourself   *good on you*

i can see   *your happiness*
the happiness   *is real this time*
in your smile!

there's a light   *you've learned*
in your eyes   *how to shine*
that wasn't there   *again*

you look   *you're no longer fighting*
so peaceful!   *yourself to survive*

it's inspiring   *your journey*
to see how far   *was worth*
you've come   *every step*

a conversation between my head and my heart

head: heart:

healing is   *healing is about*
erasing the past.   *making peace with it.*

healing means   *healing means bec-*
returning to who   *oming a fresh version*
i used to be.   *of yourself.*

i haven't   *pain won't disappear.*
healed until   *it just no longer*
it stops hurting.   *controls you.*

i need the past   *healing*
to make sense   *doesn't depend*
before i can heal.   *on understanding.*

i don't know how to start fixing myself.
you're starting in the same place
everyone else has.

are we healing?
yes. we always were.

though some of us may have similar goals,
we all have different paths
what matters most isn't the fastest route,
but the one that fits you best,
as comparison only delays your arrival

it doesn't matter if someone else takes the freeway,
while you have to weave through three exits,
when both roads still lead you home

regardless of the route,
if the destination embraces us just the same,
then the steps we take should be our own,
each stride a signature written across the earth

"maybe if i wasn't me, i would actually be happy"

for years, i drowned in self-hatred
and constant comparison,
becoming a version of myself
that was never enough
i believed everyone around me
possessed something i lacked,
from beauty, to confidence, to purpose

i distorted who i wanted to be,
turning everything around me
into mirrors for comparison
i tried to look happier on social media,
but i just became a shameful facade
of who i *really* was

i grew tired of pretending to be someone i wasn't
and chose to embrace the *real* me

i stopped trying to be better than others
and focused on being better than yesterday's me
because growth is more about becoming
than it is about achieving

there is a joy in learning to love
the parts of yourself you once neglected
your uniqueness is not something to be ashamed of
but something to be proud of
you are worth celebrating
because you are what makes you, *you*

"maybe if you weren't you,
you wouldn't have made it this far"

time really *does* heal

some wounds close like paper cuts,
quietly and unnoticed,
while others mend like broken bones,
demanding rest and patience

and still, the body knows how to recover,
like grass pushing through cracked pavement

slow healing is still healing,
and there's nothing wrong with needing more time

some wounds take twice as long to close
as they did to open,
but when they *do* heal,
you'll feel twice as strong,
twice as alive,
twice as *whole*,
more than you were before you were broken

i love all the talk about the inner child,
but what about the outer me?
the one writing resumes,
steering the wheel toward tomorrow?

what about the things i want to achieve
and the places i want to see
and the person i want to *be*?

while it is important
to avoid suppressing your inner child,
it is just as important
to honor the outer you

your inner child and outer you
should work hand in hand
to carry each other through the dark
and celebrate each other in the light

after all,
when working together,
you will both rise
in ways neither could alone

stop.
slow down.
look closer.

warning signs are not meant to be ignored
for they are quite literally a sign of things to come
painting over a warning sign
doesn't erase the danger ahead
it erases your chance to prepare

it is better to face the issue now
than crash into the problem later,
and it is better to stop at the sign
than regret where it leads

healing is pictured as an ethereal journey, an elegant masterpiece brushed onto a canvas. but no one talks about the smudges in the corners, the streaks that refuse to blend. healing requires a lot of breaking before you can even begin to rebuild.

healing requires work no one else sees, and progress that doesn't feel like progression. it demands getting out of bed even when the morning feels no different than the night. it urges you to feel everything, even when it's overwhelming. it invites you to believe change is happening, even when everything feels the same.

while healing, you are forced to immerse yourself in mornings wrapped in grief and nights without sleep. you resist the urge to run back to what hurt you because it feels familiar. you let go without closure, peace, or validation. you trust your voice, especially in the moments it usually stays silent.

there was pressure to heal quickly and quietly. people wanted to see the version of me already better. they celebrated my recovery, but ignored my reality. they asked for progress updates as if healing followed a timeline, but healing shouldn't come with a deadline.

some days, healing takes all your effort just to survive, and survival itself *is* healing. there's beauty in letting yourself *feel* instead of shutting off. there's beauty in making it through a day and saying, *i made it through the day.* there's beauty in simply *breathing.* in. and out. that's the greatest victory of all.

so yes, while it is painted as beautiful, most of the time, healing is ugly. shards cut, edges sharp, colors scattered without a pattern. but when they join together, like broken pieces forming stained glass, they bend light into radiance. proof that even fractures can glow.

many times,
closure is seen as the final chapter,
the clean break,
the last answer we need
to finally move on,
but the truth is,
when you chase closure in everything,
you're not running toward a finish line
you're just running on a treadmill

the problem with chasing closure
is that not everyone is capable of offering it
some people leave quietly
others leave marks everywhere
depending on others for closure
is like giving them the keys to your heart,
and would you leave your keys
with someone who can't even keep track of theirs?

peace doesn't have to be the closing of a story
it can be found
by learning to live with unfinished pages

closure isn't the only way to find peace
in fact, letting go of the need for closure
is what makes peace possible
sometimes,
doors are left open not to be re-entered,
but to remind you where you've already walked through

not everything that grows looks the same

a seedling grows differently
from a kitten, which grows differently
from a toddler,
but that doesn't make any of their growth
any less beautiful

so stop using another person's timeline to measure your own
instead, take comfort in knowing
you are both still healing, each in your own way

remember,
even flowers that bloom in different seasons
still reach for the same sky

sometimes, healing bruises deeper than the injury, pressing your hands over wounds you'd rather cover. and that's okay. healing doesn't begin in clarity, but in murkiness. wounds are immediate—sudden, raw, reactive. but healing is cautious—silent, timid, unpredictable.

healing asks more of us than we realize. it asks us to reopen the door to memories we locked away in the attic of our minds. it pushes us out of what feels comfortable, because pain can feel like home if we've lived in it long enough.

healing isn't linear. it doesn't follow a schedule. it isn't a puzzle that snaps into place. some days feel like progress, others like relapse, and both are part of the journey. chaos doesn't mean you're falling. it means you're human.

some wounds never fully heal. they leave scar tissue—tougher, but tender in certain light. it doesn't mean you're broken or incapable of healing. it means you've adapted and are capable of growing. it means you've found a way to live *with* your scars, not in spite of them.

the most important thing is to keep moving toward healing, no matter how small the steps. healing may not look like you imagine, but it *will* be there. one day, you'll look back and say, *i didn't even notice i was getting better. and then i realized: i was.*

to ycu

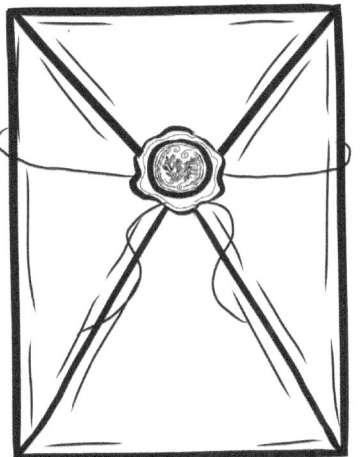

i genuinely believed that i would feel better
if i disappeared into the dark
i believed life would be better for everyone
without me,
but someone once told me something powerful
that shaped my perspective ever since:
self-destruction doesn't end the pain
it just passes it on to someone else

you may feel hurt,
and i'm sorry you do
your emotions are valid
you don't need to feel guilty for them
but i want you to know
that there are people who care about you,
who love you,
even if they don't always show it
they won't know your battles
if you don't tell them how you feel

i want you to stay strong
someone still holds their breath every time you're in pain
so please,
breathe,
for their sake,
and for yours
you matter to me,
and i want you
to start mattering to you too

you've already made it this far,
so why let turbulence drag you down?
why let small storms stall your sky?

remember all the sacrifices you made,
the fuel that carried you this far?
remember the first step,
how you longed to stand
where you are now?

even if the finish line takes longer,
or looks different than it did
when you began,
it's still worth crossing

setbacks don't erase the steps that brought you here
they carve deeper meaning into every one

broken does not mean ugly
for even broken crayons
can still create elegant masterpieces
so what's stopping you from doing the same?

don't forget,
your colors still matter,
even when they don't look perfect
after all,
even a broken crayon
will smooth itself out
after enough practice,
after patience,
with time

"hey. it's me. your inner child. i noticed that you've been suppressing yourself lately. something shifted in you. the confidence you once had has dimmed. sometimes i, the child, am steadier than you. it breaks my heart to see you go through your pain, and forget i exist.

"still, do you remember when we sat by the window with hot chocolate, watching the rain, dreaming of the future? when we used to dream big about conquering fears and chasing goals? you stopped somewhere along the way. when did fear become more trustworthy than faith? i understand the pain you carry. i carried it too. i'm sorry you went through that, and if i could have prevented it, i would have.

"but please come back to yourself. remember all the times i was proud of us for how much we'd grown. remember how we looked forward to getting bigger and wiser, so we could face our fears? well, you're bigger and wiser now.

"please come home. i've been saving your place. i'm not asking you to become someone new. be who we've always been. i never stopped believing in us. keep believing in us too. please talk to me more. i miss you.

sincerely,
you"

your experiences should not be erased,
even the ones that wrote their scars across your pages,
for they turned your story into a testimony

accept your experiences for what they are,
and release the weight of self-blame
your experiences are part of your story,
a testament to what you've overcome,
proof the battles you thought you lost
were victories all along

they remind you
you are more than what happened to you,
and there is no shame in survival

dwelling on pain does not restore you,
but turning the page does
strength is rewriting your story,
no longer letting your first draft define you

hey. it's okay. you're okay. everything will be okay. i know things are heavy right now, but it won't always be this way.

life has been hard for you. your feelings are valid. you've fought unseen battles, cried silent tears, carried the weight of loneliness too many times to count. remember: invisible doesn't mean unreal.

you've come so far, even if you can't see it. be proud of how you've persevered. things can and *will* change. you are not alone; you don't have to carry it all. you are worth more than you think. you are human, and that makes you priceless.

there will be mornings where the sun feels like it rose just for you, skies washed clean after the storm. hard days will come, but hopeful days will outnumber them. days where beauty lingers, joy returns, and peace rests with you. if there's one thing i'll leave you with, it's this: the pain you've been feeling cannot compare to the joy that is coming.

the next time you gaze at your reflection
and only see its flaws, consider this:
it's been begging you to notice the good features too

that scar you cover up?
i see it as proof that you encountered difficult trials
and came out on top

the lines beneath your eyes?
they are paragraphs
that contain every laugh,
every cry,
and every moment you survived

the spots on your skin you're ashamed of?
i see it as a personal constellation
that makes you uniquely you

you may flinch every time you see me,
but when i look at you,
i am enamored by how naturally beautiful you are
the things you love to hate
are the things i love the most

your eyes have watched your world fall and rise
there is admiration that comes with that kind of wisdom
you have always been full of life
and i never stopped seeing the light in your eyes,
even when you did

the next time you face your reflection, don't turn away.
it reflects the light that's always been there,
waiting for you to see it too.

before reading this,
i want you to press pause
on all of your thoughts.

e. hold. one. two. three. e

l   x

a   h

h   a

n   l

i   e.

feel your chest rise.
feel it fall.
feel how alive you are, right now.
now, let your breath carry these questions:

when, if ever,
was the last time you let yourself be enough
without needing to prove it?
and what would it mean
to finally start now?

don't be afraid to cry.
it's the body reminding you you're alive.
after all,
it's the first thing you did
when you entered this world.

you may have cried
after a rough heartbreak,
your heart a bridge buckling under too much weight.

your tears weren't overreactions.
they were floodwaters feeding new ground,
born from the storms you overcame.

crying isn't weakness.
strength is admitting you're not okay.
it is proof of life itself.

please don't be ashamed to cry,
for every tear you shed
is proof your soul still knows how to cleanse itself.

for every *this could have been so much better*
there is a *this could have been so much worse*

the night that steals the stars
still offers you the moon

if you live in what could have been,
you'll miss the beauty of what *is*

i. to the one who is scared of the monsters under his bed:
you don't have to be scared. the dark won't always be scary. the
shadows are not enemies, just shapes waiting for light. your
imagination and sensitivity don't make you weak; they make
you resilient. you're safe, and you'll grow braver every night. i
admire your tender heart. please don't ever lose your
innocence.

ii. to the one who is scared of the monsters around his school:
one day, the monsters left the shadows and began lurking in
the hallways. you don't have to carry that fear alone. i see the
silence you were forced to keep, and the battles you haven't
told anyone about. your worth isn't defined by what others say.
your worth was set the moment you stepped into this world. no
matter how lonely you feel, you are never alone. i admire your
endurance. please don't ever lose your persistence.

iii. to the one who is scared of the monsters within himself:
eventually, the loudest monsters were not outside, but inside.
you don't have to fear yourself. i know you've spent years
wrestling with who you are. your heart is not a battlefield. it is
a garden learning which roots to keep. be gentle with yourself.
find peace the same way you gave it to others. celebrate your
growth, even when it feels unseen. i admire your courage in
vulnerability. please don't ever lose your confidence.

iv. to the one who is no longer scared of any monsters:
the day came when the monsters disappeared altogether. i'm
proud you no longer feel scared. you carry every version of me,
and they all thank you. there are no more monsters. only
memories, and none of them own you. you are living proof that
in the end, we survived, we softened, and we soared. you are
the dream i spent my entire life praying for. i admire your
strength softened by compassion. please don't ever lose your
temperance.

sincerely,
you

i need you to do one thing.
stop trying to outrun tomorrow.
stay here.

tick–in this sentence.
tock–in this pause.
tick–in this moment.
tock–and now, listen.

tick–
you spend too much time on what you cannot fix, what you
cannot predict. you rephrase what cannot be rewritten. you
tighten your grip on things you are not meant to hold.
–*tock*.

tick–
not everything goes to plan, but that doesn't make you a
failure. it makes you human. some things fall apart so they can
fall into place differently.
–*tock*.

tick–
stop time-traveling into tomorrow. tomorrow will come with
its own weight—no need to carry it early. trust you'll have
enough strength to meet tomorrow when it comes.
–*tock*.

tick–
most things are beyond your control, so why waste your peace
on them? instead, focus on what's standing right in front of
you. right here. right now.
–*tock*.

it may feel like the end,
the quiet when the last leaf falls,
but the way winter makes room for spring,
it might just be the beginning of renewal

you thought you couldn't make it,
yet here you are,
reading this sentence.
no matter how many times life kicked you down,
you always dusted yourself off and got back up.
even your darkest nights ended with a sunrise,
and no matter how bad things got,
they always got better.
you may feel like you're not strong enough.
you may feel like everything will keep piling up,
that nothing will get better.
but i want you to know that you are strong.
you are seen,
you are known,
and you are loved.
i care about you.
i really do.
please start caring about you too.

my love.
you didn't lose them.
true loss leaves you with nothing.
but this?

this was like a bird learning to fly
after a lifetime in a cage
it gave you what you needed:
a chance to meet yourself again.

you can't earn a college degree
in one semester

you can't teach your fingers
a symphony overnight

you can't hold deep conversations
in a language you just met

and you can't rewrite your story
in just one chapter

you may be questioning why you're going through this
and how long it will last,
wondering why life feels like road signs in a foreign language,
but i promise that someday,
this will all make sense

i know it's much easier said than done,
but let the seeds do their work underground
all of your answers
are already on their way home

healing isn't demolition.
it's renovation.
you may feel like burning everything down
when you feel broken,
but with restoration,
you don't have to start over to begin reformation.
it's okay to start where you are and work toward rejuvenation.

you can begin peeling wallpaper,
shedding what no longer suits you,
and honoring what once felt like home.

you can replace broken windows
to see the world clearly again,
letting light in after seasons of darkness.

you can reinforce your foundation,
holding the parts of you that stayed solid through the storms,
rediscovering who you've always been.

you can make your home livable again,
inviting warmth,
color,
and comfort,
celebrating the life you are *living*,
not just surviving.

your home was never abandoned.
it was waiting for your return.
i hope you'll drop the matches in your hand
and replace them with safety gear as you restore your home.
you were whole once,
and you will be whole again.

you've spent a lifetime
choosing other people's desires
over your own
and though you may feel hesitant
about choosing yourself for once,

it will feel like untying the knots
that bound you for years
it will be a decision
you will never regret

the
sun

                                    t
                              h
                        g   s   d
                    i   e   l
still pulls flowers toward its l   o   r
still paints the sky with color as it g   o
still shapes the rhythm of the entire w

the way it travels
from day to night
may not look impressive to others,
but it still matters to you
                                    h
whether quickly or slowly,   g
confident or hesitant,   u
stern or gentle,   o
you are healing   n
and that's more than e

you made a mistake.
so what?
is it really the end of the world?
is it the first mistake you've ever made?
will it be the last?
of course not.
it happened.
it's done.
and you're still here.

everyone stumbles,
even those who swear they never fall.
the truth is,
nobody's perfect,
so why keep trying to be?
mistakes are just the beginning of choices,
and will you let your choices anchor you,
or ignite you?

the things we cherish most did not arrive perfect.
they were built through wrong turns,
rough drafts,
and falling down more times than they stood.
you are not defined by your mistakes,
but you can let them carve you,
shaping you into someone only brokenness could build.

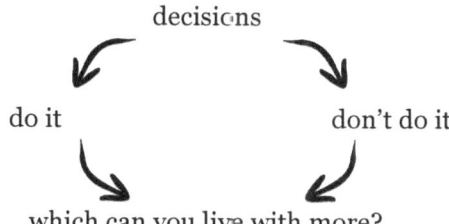

"hey. it's me. you asked me to come home, so here i am. i'm sorry. for not speaking sooner. for not showing up more. for not letting you laugh as loud as you wanted. for leaving you alone when you needed arms to cry into. i always said you disappeared for good, but the truth is you've always been here. i just never noticed.

"but even through my silence, you endured. i would not have the resilience, creativity, or hope i do without you. i know i haven't shown it, but i'm proud of your courage. i'm proud of your laughter. i'm proud of your ability to dream. most of all, i'm proud of you.

"i won't abandon you anymore. from now on, i'll make you feel seen. i'll let you laugh as loud as you want. i'll be the shoulder you cry on. we've been through so much together, hand in hand, even when i didn't squeeze back.

i promise to be here for you, as you've always been for me. you never left me, and now, i choose to stay.

finally,
you"

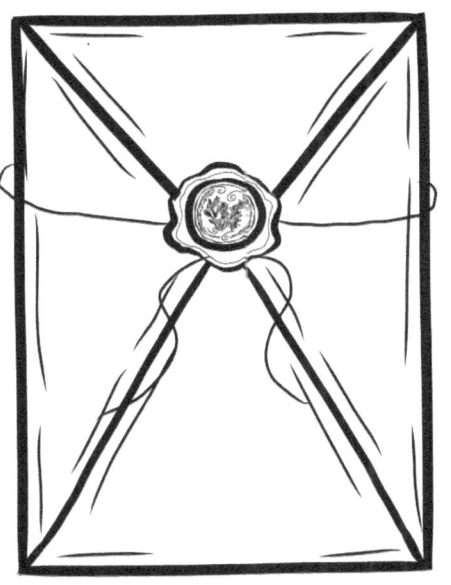

acknowledgments

to God, my Creator
You have been the constant thread woven through every
season of my life. Even when i questioned the path ahead, You
remained faithful, carrying me through the moments i could
not carry myself. every page in this book is evidence of Your
grace.

to Daisy, my other half
you gave my mind the motivation it needed when my heart
didn't want to believe in itself. your love has shaped me into
someone i never thought i could be. i would not be me if i were
not loved by you. thank you for being you.

to Shelby, my editor
you helped me uncover a voice i could not reach on my own.
your guidance has turned scattered words into something
whole and meaningful, and your encouragement has been a
light at every stage of my writing. this journey wouldn't be
possible without you.

to Karen, Katie, and Kris, my beta readers
thank you for lending not just your time, but your hearts to this
book. your honesty and belief in these poems helped refine
them into something more vulnerable and alive. each of you
pushed me to see my work from new angles, and this collection
is better because of you.

to you, my fellow traveler
thank you for opening these pages and letting me share a part
of my soul with you. if even one line spoke to your heart, then
this book has done what it was meant to do. i hope you carry
these words with you the way i carried them while writing.

connect with me!

🎵 : tonycpoetry

📷 : tonycpoetry

🌐 : tonycpoetry.com

resources

if anything in these pages felt heavy, triggering, or left you needing a little more support, you're not alone. here are some people you can reach out to, places you can visit, and lines that are always open.

mental health & crisis support
988 Suicide & Crisis Lifeline (U.S.):
call or text 988 — available 24/7
988lifeline.org

International Suicide Hotlines:
if you're outside the U.S., this site lists crisis lines by country:
findahelpline.com

abuse & domestic violence
National Domestic Violence Hotline:
call 1-800-799-SAFE (7233) or text START to 88788
thehotline.org

grief & loss
The Dougy Center — for children, teens, and families
dougy.org

whatever you're feeling—please know it's valid.
whatever you're carrying—i hope you find relief.
you made it to the end of this book, and that means something.
take care of you. the world is better with you in it.
— tony